Black Squirrels on Parade

Jane Moorman

Marysville, Kansas, is designated as a Black Squirrel City. To pay homage to the rare animal, the city's convention and tourism committee championed a public art project beginning in 2015. Five-foot tall black fiberglass squirrels. Each statue received a catchy name and was adorn in one-of-a-kind artwork by an area artist or by an artist who has ties to the area.

Seven years later, I discovered the public art project while driving through the town. I was so amazed at the artwork, so I located each and photographed all 51 statues.

Jane Moorman, photographer

Marysville honors its special residents

You never know what you are going to find when you travel the U.S. Routes, the original national highway system. Unlike the interstate system, the older routes travel through towns across the United States where there are many gems to be found.

One such highway is US 36, which follows the Pony Express route from St. Joseph, MO, to Denver, CO. In northeastern Kansas it passes through Marysville.

Prior to visiting Marysville, I learned the town was known for the black squirrels that reside in the trees of the town. I decided to stop there to see if I could photograph some of these descendants of the black morph fox squirrels. This is when I discovered the Black Squirrels on Parade.

The legend of the black squirrel's arrival to Marysville began in the 1920s as a part of an exhibit for a circus. They were accidentally released after a child opened the cage holding the animal.

Through the years Marysville residents have known the bushy-tailed black animals made their city special. There is even a city code officially designating the black squirrel as the city's mascot.

The code offers the black squirrel "all the rights and privileges inherent to such designation, including the freedom to trespass on all city property, immunity from traffic regulations, and the right for first choice to all black walnuts growing within the city."

To pay homage to the black squirrel, Marysville's Convention and Tourism committee led the charge to bring a public art project, Black Squirrels on Parade, to the city.

The project was announced in June 2015. Local people sponsored the purchase of the five-foot-tall black fiberglass squirrels. Each statue received a catchy name and was adorned with one-of-a-kind artwork by an area artist, or by an artist who has ties to the area.

Seventeen high school art students created models of their interpretation for the statue. The sculpture by Rachel Frese was chosen for the 5-foot-9-inches statue produced by America's Fiberglass Animals in Seward, NE. Owner Patrick Keough is one of a few fiberglass sculpture artists in the country.

The first 21 painted statues of the Black Squirrel Parade debuted at the city's 44th Black Squirrel Night in October 2016. In 2018, 13 more statues joined the original squirrels around the town.

In 2017, Marysville's Black Squirrel on Parade public art display won first place in the community awareness category at the Kansas Tourism Conference.

To honor the 50 years of Marysville's designation as a Black Squirrel City, additional squirrels were added in 2022 to bring the total count to 51.

The tourism committee has created a city map of the statue locations, along with a check list for visitors to record their viewings. Visitors may call 785-879-4093 while touring to learn more about each squirrel.

Jane Moorman, photographer

HELIANTHUA "Heli"

Artist
Abby Stallbaumer

Sponsor

Sunflower Community Federal
Credit Union

For more information
call (785) 879-4093(2#) to
learn more about this squirrel.

LUCY

Artist
April Spicer

Sponsor

Krammer Oil Company

For more information
call (785) 879-4093(1#) to
learn more about this squirrel.

JB CLEAN

Artist
Marissa Capp
Skylar Rhodes

Sponsor
JB Wash

For more information
call (785) 879-4093(3#) to
learn more about this squirrel

WINNIE

Artist
April Spicer

Sponsor
IdntiTeez

For more information
call (785) 879-4093(5#) to
learn more about this squirrel.

SEEGA

Artist
Dean Randolph
Aubrie (Peschel) Randolph

Sponsor
CES Group Inc

For more information
call (785) 879-4093(6#) to
learn more about this squirrel.

CALEB

Artist
April Spicer

Sponsor

Pepsi Cola Bottling Company

For more information
call (785) 879-4093(7#) to
learn more about this squirrel.

MOCHILA

Artist
Kellie Dillinger

Sponsor

Pony Express Barn and Museum

For more information
call (785) 879-4093(8#) to
learn more about this squirrel.

CHOO-CHOO

Artist
Kaci Smith

Sponsor

KNDY Radio The Marysville Advocate

For more information
call (785) 879-4093(9#) to
learn more about this squirrel.

BRICK

Artist
Aubrie Peschel

Sponsor
Marysville Main Street Big Blue BBQ
Auto Fest

For more information
call (785) 879-4093(10#) to
learn more about this squirrel.

DOTTIE ROSE

Artist
Rebecca Bricker-Smith

Sponsor
Alliance Insurance

For more information
call (785) 879-4093(11#) to learn more about this squirrel.

MAUI

Artist
AshLeigh deKoning

Sponsor
Blue River EyeCare

For more information
call (785) 879-4093(12#) to
learn more about this squirrel.

MAYOR ALONZO

Artist
Chloe Cudney

Sponsor
City of Marysville

For more information
call (785) 879-4093(15#) to
learn more about this squirrel

BEAU RISTA

Artist
Ruth Seagren

Sponsor
eMpTy Cup

For more information
call (785) 879-4093(13#) to
learn more about this squirrel.

MARTY

Artist
Madison Lynch

Sponsor

Marshal County Arts Cooperative,
Marysville Area

For more information
call (785) 879-4093(18#) to
learn more about this squirrel.

SHIRLEY

Artist
Abby Stallbaumer

Sponsor
Friends and Family of Shirley Little

For more information
call (785) 879-4093(14#) to
learn more about this squirrel.

HANS the gardener

Artist
Arlene (Brunkow) Haner

Sponsor
Kessinger Family

For more information
call (785) 879-4093(17#) to
learn more about this squirrel.

SUNNY

Artist
Samantha Dummermuth

Sponsor

Citizens State Bank

For more information
call (785) 879-4093(16#) to
learn more about this squirrel.

EVE

Artist
Patty Kahn

Sponsor
L.O.V.E. Marysville

For more information
call (785) 879-4093(20#) to
learn more about this squirrel.

FRIDA

Artist
Rita Pecenka-Brummond

Sponsor
Kessinger Family

For more information
call (785) 879-4093(32#) to
learn more about this squirrel

LA AZTECA

Artist
Ben Gordan

Sponsor

El Ranchero Mexican Restaurant

For more information
call (785) 879-4093(4#) to
learn more about this squirrel.

LILY

Artist
Willa Griswald

Sponsor
Marysville Garden Club

For more information
call (785) 879-4093(19#) to
learn more about this squirrel.

HOMER

Artist
Skylar Rhodes

Sponsor
Marysville High School Class of 2016-17

For more information
call (785) 879-4093(21#) to
learn more about this squirrel.

BIG JOHN

Artist
April Spicer

Sponsor
Bulldog Family

For more information
call (785) 879-4093(28#) to
learn more about this squirrel.

MARSHALL

Artist
Arlene Brunkow Haner

Sponsor

Cells-U-More

Brad & Sharon Ekiss

First Commerce Bank

Koester House Museum Foundation

Preceptor Zeta Chapter of Beta Sigma Phi

Loren & Gloria Smith

For more information

call (785) 879-4093(23#) to
learn more about this squirrel.

COPPER

Artist
Audrey Pilsl

Sponsor

United Bank & Trust

For more information
call (785) 879-4093(36#) to
learn more about this squirrel.

MILLIE O'NAIR
'Millionaire'

Artist
Tracy Robinson

Sponsor
The Trust Company

For more information
call (785) 879-4093(22#) to
learn more about this squirrel.

SUDSY

Artist
Connor Crist

Sponsor

Super Wash

For more information
call (785) 879-4093(31#) to
learn more about this squirrel.

SAFETY the Squirrel

Artist
Peyton Smith

Sponsor

Landoll Corporation

For more information
call (785) 879-4093(48#) to
learn more about this squirrel.

ROAD WARRIOR

Artist
April Spicer

Sponsor

Hall Brothers, Inc.

For more information
call (785) 879-4093(50#) to
learn more about this squirrel.

SIMON

Artist
Allison Manley

Sponsor
Marysville Chamber of Commerce

For more information
call (785) 879-4093(24#) to
learn more about this squirrel.

PAYNE

Artist
Patty Kahn

Sponsor
Kickhaefer and Buessing Marysville
Dental Care

For more information
call (785) 879-4093(46#) to
learn more about this squirrel

COSMO

Artist
Elizabeth Lupen

Sponsor
Landoll Lanes

For more information
call (785) 879-4093(38#) to
learn more about this squirrel.

VIOLA

Artist
Kaci Smith

Sponsor

Kracht Family Insurance

For more information
call (785) 879-4093(27#) to
learn more about this squirrel.

SISTER TERESA

Artist
April Spicer

Sponsor

Vincent J. Gentuso Jr In loving memory of his wife Teresa Schnelder Gentuso

For more information

call (785) 879-4093(29#) to learn more about this squirrel.

DEWEY

Artist
Willa Griswald

Sponsor

Marshall County Farm Bureau

Marysville Public Library

For more information
call (785) 879-4093(26#) to
learn more about this squirrel.

ED U. CATE

Artist
April Spicer

Sponsor
Marysville Elementary PTO

For more information
call (785) 879-4093(25#) to
learn more about this squirrel

RAMMY

Artist
Rebecca Luedders

Sponsor
GSLA Alumni & Association

For more information
call (785) 879-4093(34#) to
learn more about this squirrel.

RAY PEARL

Artist
Allison Manley-Lubbers

Sponsor
Venue 36

For more information
call (785) 879-4093(51#) to
learn more about this squirrel.

STUD

Artist
April Spicer

Sponsor
Argo Construction

Crome Lumber

Edwards Quarry

Ground Up Construction

Inline Construction

Latta Plumbing

Nelson Power

Rainbow International

For more information
call (785) 879-4093(30#) to
learn more about this squirrel.

PAT THE PILOT

Artist
Patrick Smith

Sponsor

Landoll Corporation

For more information
call (785) 879-4093(44#) to
learn more about this squirrel.

FREEDOM SPIRIT

Artist
Arlene Brunkow Haner

Sponsor

Kansas Army National Guard A Battery

2nd Field Artillery

For more information
call (785) 879-4093(37#) to
learn more about this squirrel.

CARL

Artist
Connor Crist

Sponsor
Cambridge Place Senior Center

For more information
call (785) 879-4093(43#) to
learn more about this squirrel.

LEO

Artist
Kristin Scheele

Sponsor

Marysville Lions Club

For more information
call (785) 879-4093(42#) to
learn more about this squirrel.

CYCLONE

Artist
Rachel Frese

Sponsor

Fresa CPA

For more information

call (785) 879-4093(39#) to
learn more about this squirrel.

SCRUBBIE

Artist
Samantha Dummermuth

Sponsor

Community Memorial Healthcare

For more information
call (785) 879-4093(40#) to
learn more about this squirrel.

CHIEF

Artist
Chloe Cudney

Sponsor

Landoll Corporation

For more information
call (785) 879-4093(41#) to
learn more about this squirrel.

PIANO BOB

Artist
Kaci Smith

Sponsor
Welch Family

For more information
call (785) 879-4093(45#) to
learn more about this squirrel.

HOPPER

Artist
April Spicer

Sponsor

Sonic Drive-In

For more information
call (785) 879-4093(35#) to
learn more about this squirrel.

SAM

Artist
Chloe Cudney

Sponsor
Walmart

For more information
call (785) 879-4093(49#) to
learn more about this squirrel.

RAZIEL

Artist
April Spicer

Sponsor
Kramer Oil Company

For more information
call (785) 879-4093(47#) to
learn more about this squirrel.

BERT

Artist
April Spicer

Sponsor
Past, Present and Future Associates
of Tenson Corporation

For more information
call (785) 879-4093(33#) to
learn more about this squirrel.

Artist and their Black Squirrels

Artist	Black Squirrel
Rebecca Bricket-Smith	DOTTIE ROSE
Arlene (Brunkow) Haner	HANS the gardener, MARSHALL, FREEDOM SPIRIT
Marissa Capp	JB CLEAN
Connor Crist	SUDSY, CARL
Chloe Cudney	MAYOR ALONZO, SAM
AshLeigh deKoning	MAUI
Kellie Dillinger	MOCHILA
Samantha Dummermuth	SUNNY, SCRUBBIE
Rachel Frese	CYCLONE
Ben Gordon	LA AZTECA
Willa Griswal	LILY, DEWEY
Patty Kahn	EVE, PAYNE (Not the name on PDF)
Rebecca Luedders	RAMMY
Elizabeth Luppen	COSMO
Madison Lynch	MARTY
Allison Manley Lubbers	SIMON, RAY PEARL
Rita Pecenka-Brummond	FRIDA
Audrey Pilsl	COPPER
Aubrie (Preschel) Randolph	SEEGA, BRICK
Dean Randolph	SEEGA
Skylar Rhodes	JB CLEAN, HOMER
Tracy Robinson	MILLIE O'HAIR "Millionaire"
Kristin Scheele	LEO
Ruth Seagren	BEAU RISTA, CHIEF
Kaci Smith	VIOLA, CHOO-CHOO, PIANO BOB
Patrick Smith	PAT the Pilot
Peyton Smith	SAFETY the Squirrel
Abby Stallbaumer	HELIAHTHUA "Heli,' SHIRLEY
April Spicer	LUCY, WINNIE, BIG JOHN, ROAD WARRIOR, SISTER TERESA ED U. CATE, STUD, HOPPER, RAZIEL, BERT, CALEB

About the Photographer

Jane Moorman describes herself as an adventurer who loves to drive the backroads to see what there is to see. During her 30-year journalism career, Jane honed her photograph skills as a photojournalist, including covering high school sporting events. A friend once said, "I wish I could see the world as Jane sees it. Finding the beauty in things that most of us don't take time to see." Her plans to travel the world after retiring was postponed by the COVID-19 pandemic. While that dream was on hold, Jane's wanderlust did not stop. Upon retiring in 2021, Jane decided there is a lot of her native country she had not visited, so began her journey of exploring the USA. She has traveled the United States coastal road along the Great Lakes, visiting 101 lighthouses. For another project she is visiting each state's capitol to photograph their uniqueness. She currently lives in Albuquerque, New Mexico, but says her real home is on the road.